MW00883751

Forest Wildlife
Coloring Book

An Adult Coloring Book Featuring Beautiful Forest Animals, Birds, Plants and Wildlife for Stress Relief and Relaxation

Copyright 2019 © Coloring Book Cafe

All Rights Reserved.

Copyright @ 2019 Coloring Book Cafe
All Rights Reserved.

All rights reserved. No part of this publication may be reproduced or used in any form or by any means--graphic, electronic, or mechanical, including photocopying, recording, or information storage-and-retrieval--without permission of the publisher.

The designs in this book are intended for the personal, noncommercial use of the retail purchaser and are under federal copyright laws; they are not to be reproduced in any form for commercial use. Permission is granted to photocopy content for the personal use of the retail purchaser.

an Imprint of **The Fruitful Mind Publishing LTD.**
www.coloringbookcafe.com

Have questions? Let us know.
support@coloringbookcafe.com

 facebook.com/coloringbookcafe @coloringbookcafe

This Book
Belongs To:

Badger

Bat

Bears

Beaver

Boar

Bobcat

Deer

Eagle

Forest Lion

Fox

Gopher

Hedgehog

Ladybug

Mushroom Mouse

Moose

Nest

Opossum

Otter

Owl

Pangolin

Rabbit

Racoon

Squirrel

Wolf

Woodpecker

Made in the USA
Columbia, SC
12 January 2023

10176800R00030